BUSINESS CREATIVITY

A Guide for Managers

Paul Birch and Brian Clegg

KOGAN PAGE

First published in 1995

Kogan Page Limited
120 Pentonville Road
London N1 9JN

British Library Cataloguing in Publication Data

A CIP record for this book is available from the British Library.

ISBN 0–7494–1638–6

Printed and bound in Great Britain by
Biddles Ltd, Guildford and King's Lynn

6·99

Short Loan Collection

south essex college
FURTHER & HIGHER EDUCATION

This book is to be returned on or before the last date stamped below.

Fines will be charged for late return at 25p per day

7 DAY BOOK

Renewals
Basildon : 01268 461641   **Southend**: 01702 220447
Thurrock: 01375 362691
or email renewals@southessex.ac.uk

30130504166961

OR
3/97

658.
403
20
BIR
SHL

658.4063BIR

Better Management Skills

This highly popular range of inexpensive paperbacks covers all areas of basic management. Practical, easy to read and instantly accessible, these guides will help managers to improve their business or communication skills. Those marked * are available on audio cassette.

The books in this series can be tailored to specific company requirements. For further details, please contact the publisher, Kogan Page, telephone 0171-278 0433, fax 0171-837 6348.

Be a Successful Supervisor
Business Etiquette
Coaching Your Employees
Creative Decision-making
Creative Thinking in Business
Delegating for Results
Effective Employee Participation
Effective Meeting Skills
Effective Performance Appraisals*
Effective Presentation Skills
Empowerment
First Time Supervisor
Get Organised!
Goals and Goal Setting
How to Communicate Effectively*
How to Develop a Positive
    Attitude*
How to Develop Assertiveness
How to Motivate People*
How to Understand Financial
    Statements
How to Write a Staff Manual
Improving Employee
    Performance
Improving Relations at Work
Keeping Customers for Life
Leadership Skills for Women

Learning to Lead
Make Every Minute Count*
Managing Disagreement
    Constructively
Managing Organisational Change
Managing Part-Time Employees
Managing Quality Customer
    Service
Managing Your Boss
Marketing for Success
Memory Skills in Business
Mentoring
Office Management
Productive Planning
Project Management
Quality Customer Service
Rate Your Skills as a Manager
Sales Training Basics
Self-managing Teams
Selling Professionally
Speed Reading in Business
Successful Negotiation
Successful Telephone Techniques
Systematic Problem-solving and
    Decision-making
Team Building
Training Methods that Work

Contents

Creativity as a Boost for Business   **7**

1.   **What Is Creativity?**   **9**
Creativity types *9*
The creative fork *11*
Obstacles to creativity *13*
The creative pickaxe *15*

2.   **A Creative Frame of Mind**   **17**
Five finger exercise 1: Reducing mailing costs *17*
Five finger exercise 2: A new paint product *18*
Five finger exercise 3: Improving customer service *21*
What have you achieved? *22*

3.   **To Boldly Go**   **23**
Step 1: Information survey *24*
Step 2: Building a solution *24*
Step 3: Reality check *24*
Step 4: Implementation *25*
It's only a little problem *25*

4.   **Step 1: Information Surveying**   **27**
The lie of the land *27*
Problem statement *28*
Why? *30*
The obstacle map *32*

The level chain *34*
The aerial survey *36*
Information surveying in action *38*

5. **Step 2: Building a Solution** 39
   Getting around obstacles *39*
   Challenging assumptions *41*
   Distortion *43*
   Reversal *45*
   Fantasy *46*
   Someone else's view *49*
   Metaphor *50*
   Random word *52*
   Random picture *54*
   A different solution *55*
   Solution building in action *56*

6. **Step 3: Reality Check** 59
   Gut feel *59*
   Stakeholders *60*
   Plus points *62*
   Minus points *63*
   Reality check in action *64*

7. **Step 4: Implementation** 65
   No application, no creativity *65*
   Implementation style *66*
   The implementation toolkit *68*
   Implementation in action *75*
   The whole implementation *78*

8. **Regular Creativity** 79
   Creativity-driven exercise *79*
   Problem-driven exercise *80*
   A checklist *80*
   And finally ... *81*

References 85

Creativity as a Boost for Business

Creativity and business can seem uncomfortable bedfellows, particularly given the popular image of creativity as an uncontrolled force, striking randomly to inspire the chosen few. There is a temptation to forget creativity and leave it to the arty types, relying on imitation of past successes and 'if it works, don't fix it' to carry business forward.

This is acceptable if competition is insignificant, if there are no obstacles in your path, and if customers are fighting to get hold of your products – but that is rarely a realistic picture. Properly structured, creativity is a business tool which can be used both to generate original ideas and to solve problems which are blocking progress.

Business creativity is not about change for its own sake. It is a means of differentiating your business and products from the competition, or of finding a solution to a problem which cannot be resolved by following the well-trodden paths of history.

To many of us, creativity does not come naturally. We are aware of a few individuals whom we can label 'creative', but do not feel ourselves capable of new and original thinking. In part this is self-preservation. If we were innovative about every act, we would never get anything done. The smooth flow of life depends on the presence of a solid foundation of habit and good practice. Yet important decisions and new ideas need a stronger basis than the repetition of past actions.

Luckily, techniques can be learned to develop creativity in all of us. This is not an approach for the specialist few, but for all business decision makers and problem solvers.

The reality of business today is that you need to be in a position to make use of creativity techniques. Business guru Tom Peters has suggested that creativity and zest are the principal originators of economic value. The techniques we will introduce you to in *Business Creativity* will help you to increase your creativity, spice up your ideas, and hence increase the value of your business.

There are various mechanisms available for stimulating creativity, some linking back to the creative arts, where a writer may adopt a particular approach to come up with a new plot line, others based on concepts developed by psychologists and those interested in the workings of the brain. While these techniques are valuable in their own right, they can be difficult to remember and are rarely used. This short book provides a strong framework for the systematic application of creativity to business.

CHAPTER 1
What Is Creativity?

Creativity types

To use creativity techniques effectively, it is important to be aware of the nature of the beast. Creativity itself is not a single process. It comprises a number of different strands, one or more of which will be involved in any act of innovation.

List below six activities you regard as creative.

1. _____

2. _____

3. _____

4. _____

5. _____

6. _____

Arthur Koestler, an early worker in the field of creativity, considers the three domains of creativity to be humour, discovery and art. They could be described as Ha Ha!, Aha! and Aaahh!.

Ha Ha!

An area which is often forgotten in discussions of creativity, but one which is of fundamental importance, is humour. Most humour works because of a re-association of familiar ideas – a fair description of the mechanics of creativity. Much of the progress made in brainstorming sessions happens when the individuals involved let go of their normal restraints and start to look at issues from a novel or amusing perspective. It is during the evaluation of creative ideas that one needs to be serious, not in their generation.

Aha!

This is the standard picture of creative thought in the business world. The inspiration which allows us to see something from a different perspective: the new invention or the enhanced product. The light bulb going on over the head. This form of creativity is associated with problem solving, where a problem is any gap between how things are and how you want them to be. The Aha! solution closes this gap at a stroke.

Aaahh!

The area of artistic creativity: a painting, a sculpture, a well-designed page layout would fall within this category. Creative design can result in people wanting to read or use a product which would otherwise be too uninspiring to bother with. Creativity increases usability, which increases effectiveness.

Your creative activities

Go back to your list of creative activities on page 9 and see which of the three creativity types were involved in each activity. Did you focus more on one form than another? The boundaries between the three types are often blurred. You may find that more than one of the above is in play at once. Could you broaden your creative base by seeing a wider range of creative possibilities? If these are the sort of activities which involve creativity, who are the most creative people? On the following list, rate each of the jobs between 1 (not very creative) and 5 (very creative):

Airline pilot —————
Ballet dancer —————
Accountant —————
Novel writer —————
Brain surgeon —————
Police constable —————
Graphic designer —————

It is quite likely that you will have rated the airline pilot low; it is certainly very desirable that pilots do not look for creative new ways of flying aircraft — upside down, for instance. However, it is equally important that when the unusual strikes, the pilot should be able to come up with innovative ways of solving the problem.

At first sight, the ballet dancer may be considered creative, but in fact this job is probably among the least creative on the list, fitting within a very fixed regime, where a set performance is repeated every night. Even a writer or graphic designer will be constrained by their genre, their target, fashion and their habitual approach. On the other hand, other, seemingly limited professions, require a very flexible, innovative attitude.

What emerges is that pigeonholing a job or type of person against a certain level of creativity is not particularly useful. This is especially true because practically any profession will benefit from properly applied creativity, and every individual is capable of improving their personal creativity by the use of the techniques we will be covering.

The creative fork

If you have any doubts about your own remarkable creativity, try the following exercise. Take two minutes (no more) to write in the box overleaf all the uses you can make of a fork.

Now take a further two minutes to write in the second box everything you can't do with a fork.

If you are a normal, warm-blooded, rational human being, it is likely that you came up with more examples in the second exercise than in the first. Now, go back to the things you said that you couldn't do with a fork. Assume that you can have a fork as big as you like (or as small as you like), that it can be made of any substance, at any temperature, and that it can be processed in any way you like. If you work at it, there will be few, if any, examples that you cannot turn around. If there are any which you really believe cannot be done, then get someone else to look at them for you.

It is clear that you could have come up with more ideas in the first exercise merely by thinking of all the uses for any object and then, later, justifying them as uses for the fork. If this looks like cheating, that's exactly the point. Creativity almost always looks like cheating. There is nothing in the original instructions which specifies size, material or processing. You placed these limitations upon yourself. This is often the way with creativity.

We limit our own ability to think creatively by making assumptions which we have no need to make. The essence of creative thinking is moving beyond these self-imposed limits to the areas where we start cheating or making fun of the subject. We then come up with solutions which break the current rules, but which may still be valid.

Obstacles to creativity

In the previous exercise, we found that our assumptions about the nature of forks were getting in the way of generating a creative solution. There are other obstacles too.

It is now widely known that the brain is divided into two halves, with the left handling sequential thought, speech and those functions generally regarded as scientific. The right half is responsible for holistic thought, images and those functions generally regarded as artistic. Even without the linkage of these tendencies to the sides of the brain – and there is some debate on the validity of this – it is clear that these two modes of thought work in very different ways.

We are taught by the school system and our socialisation to rely more heavily on the left-hand side of the brain than the right. In many, this reliance moves to the point where they find it difficult to use the right-hand side of the brain to any degree, and instead they use the left for functions to which it is ill suited.

Creativity is a whole brain function. The right brain is needed to move from traditional, well-trodden paths into new areas which at first appear irrational. The left brain is needed to evaluate ideas and to develop those which are most workable. Using all of your brain can be hard work when you are not used to it. As with any form of exertion, exercise is good for you. The more you work at being creative, the easier it becomes.

As we have already seen with the fork exercise, preconceptions and assumptions box in our creativity. From our first understanding of speech we are bombarded with restrictions. Tick any of the statements below which you have heard being used to suppress an idea. You may even have used a few yourself:

1. We don't do things that way here. ☐
2. We tried it before and it didn't work. ☐
3. That's not the right answer. ☐
4. It wouldn't work in practice. ☐
5. It's not my (his, her) area. ☐
6. Don't be silly. ☐
7. That would break the rules. ☐
8. We can't take the risk. ☐

Now, on the lines below, list some other idea-killers you may have heard or used.

_____

_____

_____

_____

_____

_____

These obstacles to new ideas are perfectly valid, but they uproot originality while it is still a tiny shoot. All the time the forces of habit and training are pushing us back into our conventional approach. Eventually, we will have to fit within some rules, but to begin with it is necessary to break out of the old mind-set.

The creative pickaxe

Some while ago we were at a school, running a creativity session with a group of 12-year-olds. They had no trouble with the concept of being locked into a tunnel of sameness, without original solutions, but most of the class could not grasp the idea of a creativity technique as a way of changing things. One of the children came up with the picture of a pickaxe. A creative pickaxe to hack your way out of the old ways of doing things on to a new path. This is a very effective image to describe what is needed: wielding the pickaxe of creativity to get out of the tunnel of stalled ideas.

Now let's move on to practise using the creative pickaxe and developing a creative frame of mind.

CHAPTER 2
A Creative Frame of Mind

The fork exercise in Chapter 1 was our first application of a creativity technique. In this chapter there are three further exercises, each using a different approach. Their purpose is to help you get into a creative frame of mind, not to learn the specific techniques, which will be slotted into a simple, four-stage framework in the rest of the book.

It is important that you do try these exercises. Each will only take around five minutes, but they form an important preparation which will make it easier to absorb the principles of business creativity. They are warm-up exercises, such as a singer or pianist might employ before launching into a full-scale performance.

Five finger exercise 1: Reducing mailing costs

Very few businesses escape the costs of mailing. In this exercise we will use a technique to tunnel through the obstacles which are in the way of achieving our goal. Just to clear your immediate thoughts, try to think of two ways you could save on mailing costs today:

1. _____

2. _____

Now forget those. Consider the business of mailing. How could things be different if the mail company paid you for the privilege of carrying your mail? List some implications of such a policy (we've filled in one example). Think of what it means for you and how the mail company would make it work in practice:

1. **You would try to post other people's mail for them**.

2. _____

3. _____

4. _____

5. _____

6. _____

7. _____

Now consider how these implications of an unlikely possibility might apply to your real problem. With our example, you might go into the mail business yourself, or you might get together with other firms to obtain a group discount from the mail company, or you might ensure that your billing is accurate and you aren't paying for someone else's mail.

Look at your list, and for each item think of a couple of ways of reducing your mail costs. Among your list there are probably some impractical suggestions, but at this point we are only generating starting points, not final solutions.

Whether you are glowing with success, or found that exercise unfruitful, let's try a totally different approach to a totally different problem.

Five finger exercise 2: A new paint product

Imagine you run a paint company. Once you have achieved a

certain quality standard and an adequate colour range, there are limits to how you can differentiate your product from the competition. In this exercise you will use the *level chain technique*, so called because it works by comparing different levels of objects or concepts in a chain. This approach takes a few moments to grasp, but is extremely powerful for exploratory work.

Starting from your current product, a can of paint, you will move up and down levels until you reach a new idea. Moving up a level involves moving to a greater degree of abstraction. If our start point is a can of paint, we could move up to a liquid, or to a pigment, or to a tin can – any more general concept which a can of paint is part of.

Moving down a level involves getting more specific. From a can of paint we could move to a can of blue paint, or a spray can of paint, or a dried-up can of paint. In forming a chain of images which will lead to your final idea, you can move up and down levels as you like. Try it now. On the lines below the starting idea, write a concept which is higher or lower in level than the previous one. Stop when you run out of lines, or you've hit on an idea that might be useful.

A can of paint

_____

_____

_____

_____

_____

_____

_____

Does it make sense? Before we ask you to make a few more such chains, here's one we made earlier:

A can of paint (up to)
Liquid (down to)
Beer (down to)
Ring-pull can of beer

At this point, a practical idea emerged. Why not sell paint in ring-pull cans? It would benefit the consumer, as ordinary paint cans are hard to open, and it would benefit the manufacturer, as customers would tend to throw away any paint left in the can and so have to buy more. We need not have stopped at that point. There is no specific right answer; we are simply looking for the inspiration which will point us in a fruitful direction. Now try again. Do two more chains:

A can of paint   **A can of paint**

_____   _____

_____   _____

_____   _____

_____   _____

_____   _____

_____   _____

If you found that exercise interesting, stop now and think of a problem that's bothering you, anything that involves finding a new product or a new way of doing something, and try this technique on it. You will find that it becomes much easier with practice.

Five finger exercise 3: Improving customer service

Many businesses thrive or die on their customer service. In this exercise, looking at customer service in a television showroom, you will use one of the techniques that overcomes the obstacles you unconsciously place in the way of finding a solution. This approach is related to the old joke about the lost driver who asks the way and is told, 'Well, if you want to get there, I wouldn't start from here.' Normally, working in a television showroom, you would look at the problem from the point of view of a salesperson or a customer. What if someone totally outside the sphere of the business were involved instead?

Pick a character from history (or historical fiction), or imagine an archetypal person of a particular period. It doesn't matter who or when, provided you have pre-dated television, and this is a person, character or type around whom you can form a strong image. Write down who it is:

_____

Now, imagine this person was suddenly plunged into selling television sets to people of his or her own age. How would they do it? What would they use to sell the product? What comparisons would they make? What programmes might they watch in their historical period? Note a few of their key selling points:

1. _____

2. _____

3. _____

4. _____

5. _____

6. _____

Think how these points might influence customer service in a present-day television shop. How could they be used to make the difference which would bring a customer into the shop?

What have you achieved?

Notice how the process you went through in the exercises, though not directly working on the problem, resulted in a wider range of possibilities. This is the pickaxe at work. The creativity technique has burst through the tunnel of conventional thought.

In itself, this is impressive, but often a randomly selected technique will not result in a usable idea. We will now look at a framework for making creativity deliver.

CHAPTER 3
To Boldly Go

In the five finger exercises you will have begun to get a feeling for the power of creativity techniques. In effect, they are levers for the brain, opening up and magnifying your own creative capabilities. But having techniques in themselves does not deliver a solution. It is not enough to generate a good idea; to make creativity deliver we have, like the characters in Star Trek, to boldly go into the unknown – to make something happen.

One of the principal problems facing anyone with a newly learned technique is keeping up its use. On the lines below write down the last three training courses you have undertaken, or business books you have read.

_____ ☐

_____ ☐

_____ ☐

Now, in the box alongside each line estimate the percentage of what you learned that you put into regular use. Many people, if honest, will score worse than 50 per cent overall. Some will come close to zero. It is an unfortunate truth that we often finish a book or come back from a course filled with enthusiasm for a newly learned approach, only to find it rapidly disappearing into the swamp of everyday practicality.

While it would probably be mildly interesting to find out about creativity but never employ the techniques, we are enthusiastic that you put them into practice. For your own part, this will only happen if you use the techniques in this book regularly. The techniques themselves are not particularly original. You will find some of them, particularly those in Step 2, in other books on creativity. But to help you to recall the process, we have put them together in a simple, four-stage framework. In any particular application it may not be necessary to use the whole structure, but by having a framework it is easy to find the appropriate techniques and slot them into place.

Step 1: Information survey

'Fools rush in where angels fear to tread' is an apt aphorism for decision makers, problem solvers and those faced with generating creative ideas. It is all too easy to suppose that you know all there is to know about the problem area. As a result of this, you can rush in, develop a solution and sit back with pride, only to find that you have solved entirely the wrong problem.

As a first step to achieving a creative business solution we need to establish what we are trying to achieve, at the same time looking for any external factors which might influence the outcome.

Step 2: Building a solution

Once the goal is clear, we can use the idea-generating creativity techniques to come up with possible solutions.

Step 3: Reality check

The output from an idea-generation session is often a significant distance from being a perfect, honed solution. In the third stage we look at how the suggested solution will affect the stakeholders in the problem area, consider the good and bad points of our idea, and establish a personal gut feeling as to the quality of this approach.

Step 4: Implementation

After honing our solution, it is put into practice. Of the four steps, this is probably the most dangerous; many good ideas have failed due to poor implementation. This is partly because little attention has been paid to the different types of problem, which can require significantly varied approaches. It is also true that the implementation phase lacks the excitement of generating a flurry of ideas. Nonetheless, a good implementation is essential to make creativity of value.

It's only a little problem

It may seem that this four-step structure is something of an obstacle itself when dealing with a problem which is not worthy of a significant effort. But this is not a rigid set of steps to be doggedly worked through at length in each and every case – that would certainly be an inappropriate sledgehammer for some nuts. Nevertheless, any problem or task will benefit from a fleeting visit to each of the four stages.

Step 1. Are we sure what our goal is? Have we got the right information?
Step 2. A quick use of a technique, perhaps taking two or three minutes.
Step 3. Bringing the output of the technique into a practical form.
Step 4. Putting the solution into practice.

For a quick problem the whole process could be undertaken in five to ten minutes: hardly a major burden, but generating a fresh, effective approach.

In the following chapters we will cover each of the four steps in detail, looking at the techniques which are available and how to apply them.

CHAPTER 4

Step 1: Information Surveying

South East Essex College
of Arts & Technology
Carnarvon Road Southend-on-Sea Essex SS2 6LS
Tel: (01702) 220400 Fax: (01702) 432320 Minicom: (01702) 220642

The lie of the land

Most people in business like to get things done. True, there are a few pen-pushers whose only aim is to get through the day with the minimum effort, but the vast majority – certainly anyone who would buy a book like this – want to be doing, not planning. This inevitably tends to push preparation to one side. But that is a mistake if creativity is to be properly applied.

The first step in the creativity process is to make sure that we know what the problem actually is, and what external influences may affect the solution. A problem is a gap between the way things are and the way you would like them to be. If you have not found such a gap, then you are yet to identify your problems – it doesn't mean that you haven't got any.

For some gaps there will never be a realistic solution. You might, for instance, hate flying, yet need to get half way across the world in a few hours. In your ideal state, you would be able to get to your destination without travelling. Just defining the gap does not solve it, but the chances are that without doing so explicitly you would have been looking at the wrong problem.

It would be easy to see the meeting or conference you must attend as the problem rather than the travelling. Taking a different viewpoint might allow you to develop an alternative solution. For instance, if you saw the meeting as your problem, you would tend to look for options which avoided the meeting. If you saw travelling as your problem, you could look for new approaches which avoided flying. Could the other participants come to you? Could you use video conferencing, or even telephone conferencing, instead of meeting face to face? A large part of the first step to creativity is identifying what your problem is and the area in which a solution might lie.

The five techniques in this chapter provide a toolbox for sorting out the mess of information which surrounds and obscures a problem. By themselves they won't provide you with a creative solution, but they will help you to understand the problem and its environment, increasing the chance that the solution you develop will be both novel and useful. Let's look at the techniques first, then pull them together in a typical application.

We begin by identifying the problem, and refining it into a clear form. In some cases, this will present itself as an obstacle to overcome; in others we need to come up with a new concept. There is an appropriate technique for each requirement. Finally, we will look at the various influences on the problem area in preparation for building a solution. Remember that each technique does not have to be worked through mechanically – this is a toolbox, not a production line, and only the appropriate tools need be selected.

Problem statement

It is essential that you have a clear statement of your problem.

To do this, merely use the words, 'How to ...' followed by a pithy description of what you need to achieve. This could be applied to our first five finger exercise, describing the problem as 'how to reduce mailing costs'. In general, it is best to develop several concise, action-oriented statements with a single problem per statement. In that same example, we could equally have said 'how to cut communications costs' or 'how to reduce mailshot costs', depending on the company.

Try taking two or three of the problems which you have at the moment, and produce some problem statements in this form. Write more than one statement for each problem.

How to_____

_____

How to_____

_____

How to_____

_____

How to_____

_____

How to_____

_____

How to_____

_____

It might seem that, with the problem identified, we are ready to roll up our sleeves and get on with the solution. Unfortunately, we are not yet adequately prepared. It is too easy to launch yourself at the wrong problem. Our next technique will test the metal of our problem statements, refining them to something more appropriate.

Why?

The technique which will test the validity of our problem statements is surprisingly effective. All you have to do is to ask, 'Why?', refining your goal and focusing in on the core of the problem.

In practice this is simply a matter of asking 'Why?' in respect of your problem statement, and then asking it again in response to the answer you generate. Repeat this process several times.

We have all heard of experienced three-year-old children asking, 'Why?' over and over again until their parents finally resort to answering, 'Because I say so!' This technique allows you to be that three-year-old. As an example, here is an imaginary problem:

How to improve the quality of my work.
Why?
Because my boss is always nagging me about it.
Why?
Because I don't follow the same sets of rules as her. I don't necessarily get in early, I don't wear a suit, but I always get the job done well.
Why?
Because I feel that the outputs I produce are more important than the way I go about producing them.
Why?
Because I am paid to produce, not to worry about an arbitrary set of rules regarding the way I do it.

It is becoming clear that the person stating the problem thinks that the outputs of the job are fundamental to success, while the boss is at least as interested in the inputs which determine the way the job is done. The problem could be restated as:

How to make my boss think that my outputs are more important than inputs.

At this stage you could go through the whole process again if you need a fuller understanding, but don't overdo it. This is a quick technique aimed at helping you to establish your bearings.

Now try it for yourself using one of your problem statements from the previous exercise.

Problem statement: How to_____

_____

Why?_____

_____

Why?_____

_____

Why?_____

_____

Why?_____

_____

Possible restatement of problem: How to _____

_____

You might like to repeat this process for the other problem statements you listed. Some will not change, but others, like the example above, will end up with quite a different problem to the one you originally envisaged.

If the problem is essentially one of overcoming an obstacle, try producing an obstacle map (see page 33), which will broaden the information in your problem statement ready to work on a solution. If, on the other hand, this is essentially a problem of new ideas — a new product for the line, a new way of doing something — try using the level chain technique (see page 34), which will either generate a new form of the problem or a solution. In either case, consider performing an aerial survey (see page 36) before proceeding with building a solution.

The obstacle map

If your problem is one of overcoming obstacles — people, processes, anything which gets in the way of making things the way you want them to be — the first requirement is to size up the opposition, a process which can be facilitated with an obstacle map as show in Figure 4.1.

Take three of your problem statements. Express them in terms of the way things are and the way you would like them to be. At this stage, don't worry about realistic wants, and don't worry about working towards solutions. Just state your problems. For the moment ignore the circle in the centre; only fill in the outer boxes.

Having summarised the way things are and the way you would like them to be, think about what is stopping you from achieving your goals. Go back to each example and write in the central circle any obstacles you can see. Don't try to move on to solutions to your problems or remove the obstacles at this stage; you are simply describing the world.

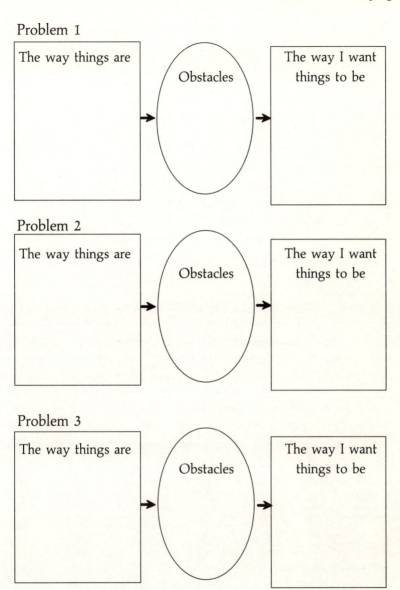

Figure 4.1 *Three obstacle maps*

Very often the act of drawing up an obstacle map can inspire you to think of solutions. If this is not the case, don't worry. The obstacle map will provide valuable input when you come to fit a solution. Drawing an obstacle map may seem a facile act, but by writing down what our goals are, and what's getting in the way, we have added extra weight to the problem statement.

That's fine if we are using creativity to overcome an obstacle, but what if we want to come up with a new concept – a new product, perhaps? It would be possible to classify the lack of a new product as our obstacle, but that is rather twisted logic. Instead, we can employ the level chain.

The level chain

Although specific in application, this is probably the most powerful technique in the information survey. This technique, which we used earlier in the paint product example on pages 19–20, builds on the fact that we are continually classifying, organising and structuring the world in which we live. We tend to see things in sets, sub-sets and super-sets. This can be an obstacle to creativity if the structure becomes too rigid and we cannot get away from it. On the other hand, we can exploit it as a mechanism for forcing movement. In the level chain we use a series of related concepts to move from an existing state to a new one.

An example will make this clearer. Imagine that we are looking for a new way of distributing milk, starting from a milk bottle. The level chain process might be:

Milk bottle (up a level to)
Container (down a level to)
Tupperware container (up a level to)
Resealable containers (down a level to)
Resealable milk bottles

In each case we move to a greater or lesser level of abstraction. The direction is purely arbitrary – the first idea that comes to mind. The process stops when you achieve what seems to be an effective goal – in this case, how to create a resealable milk bottle.

Now it's your turn to try examples based on idea generation and problem solving. First, start by finding a new and original way of fastening clothes starting from the principle of a button. Each time, move up or down a level of generality until you hit on an idea that appeals to you.

Button

_____

_____

_____

_____

_____

_____

If you found this difficult, do not give up. Try again. This technique can provide powerful new insights to your problem and becomes much easier with practice.

When the level chain is used, it may be possible to skip over the second step in the four-step process. We have already applied a powerful creativity technique and may not need to build a new solution. If that is the case, consider applying an aerial survey, then go on to step three, the reality check.

But the outcome of the level chain can be a goal rather than a solution in itself. In the milk bottle example, we now have the new problem, 'how to create a resealable milk bottle', to overcome. If we have generated a new problem, it is worth using the 'Why?' technique to make sure that we are addressing the right problem, and the obstacle map if appropriate, then considering an aerial survey before going on to step two.

The aerial survey

An aerial survey is extremely valuable for larger scale problems. It provides an overview, allowing you to rise above your problem area like a helicopter to see just what is liable to have an influence – good or bad – on your solution. The technique used here is *mind mapping*, first developed by Tony Buzan in the early 1970s. It involves a pictorial representation of a subject rather than traditional linear notes.

To draw a mind map, start with your page turned to landscape (with the longest side top and bottom rather than left and right) and put an image in the middle which represents the subject of the map. The main subdivisions of the subject radiate out from this central image and then themselves divide organically into smaller and smaller branches. Figure 4.2 gives an example of a mind map for business creativity.

The mind maps which you are going to draw are maps of the mess which surrounds your problem. Drawing the map allows you to see what is known, to structure your thinking, and also to highlight areas where your understanding is inadequate.

Try producing an aerial survey of any one of the problems that you wrote above in the obstacle maps. Pick the most complex or difficult one. Take a blank sheet of paper turned to landscape and draw a small image of the problem in the centre. You don't have to be Leonardo da Vinci to make this work. The image is there for your benefit, no one else's.

Next, draw a thick line (a branch or root) from the central image and write along it a keyword representing a sub-area of the problem. Anything you write on a mind map should be either a picture or a simple keyword. Do not use sentences.

Now you can add lower level subdivisions of this area or, if another broad concept occurs to you, start another branch

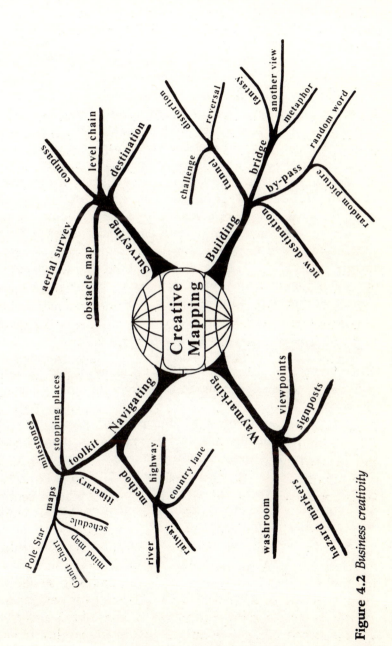

Figure 4.2 *Business creativity*

from the centre. In general, try to draw lines like the branches of a tree. Draw thick supporting branches near the centre and move out to increasingly thinner ones near the edge.

Once you have finished the map, you have completed the bulk of the work of the aerial survey. The next stage is simply to use the map to gain a better understanding of what you know and what you don't know. Study your map and see if there are associations which had not occurred to you before. Are there gaps in your understanding? Are there, for instance, branches which should be heavy with twigs but which you have left bare? Are there branches missing? The map's initial use ends here, but it will continue to be a point of reference throughout the four steps of the creative process.

If you are dealing with a very large project, you may want to redraw your first map to tidy up relationships, correct mistakes and add any omissions. You might also add more images and colour. These are not as necessary for an aerial survey as they are for a mind map aimed at helping you to remember a subject, but they can be fun.

Information surveying in action

Once you are familiar with the five techniques in the toolbox, it is easy to apply them appropriately in any particular situation.

Make sure you have stated your problem as one or more pithy 'how to' statements. Refine your problem statement by asking 'Why?'. Decide whether you are overcoming an obstacle or generating a new concept — draw up an obstacle map or use the level chain. If the problem is significant, make sure you understand the context and influences of the problem with an aerial survey.

Having done this, you are ready to move on to generating a solution.

CHAPTER 5

Step 2: Building a Solution

Getting around obstacles

In this chapter we move into the field which most people associate with creative problem solving: the techniques of innovation. One last word of caution, though: don't rush into attempting to solve the problem too quickly. Make sure that you have used the information surveying techniques to establish what your problem really is.

Traditional, logical problem solving looks for likely, direct solutions. In effect, it tries to find a way to remove obstacles. Creative problem solving looks for more varied ways to avoid obstacles. The techniques we will use are designed to break away from conventional thought, often coming at an obstacle from a totally different direction or circumventing it entirely. Depending upon the size or complexity of the problem you face, you would typically employ one or two of these techniques. For particularly knotty problems you might want to use more.

Look back at the obstacle maps you drew at the start of the previous chapter. In between 'the way things are' and 'the way you would like things to be', you wrote a list of obstacles. What can you do to cope with those obstacles? The ideas you generate will range from the mundane to the novel, from the possible to the impossible. In general, the more novel an idea,

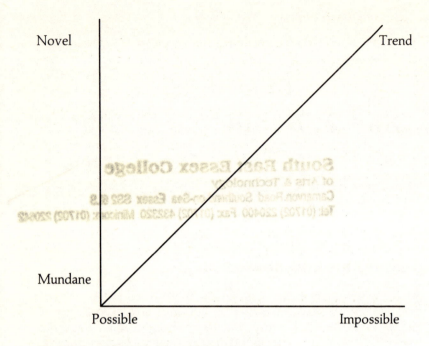

Figure 5.1 Novelty/Possibility graph

the more likely it is to move towards the impossible. There is a trend, as shown in Figure 5.1.

Very often obstacles occur because your desired final state is novel and, therefore, tends towards the impossible. The usual approach to solving such a problem is to tackle the obstacle head on. The creative approach is more indirect, but almost always more effective.

Once you have drawn an obstacle map you will have a feel for the size of the obstacles you face. If they are small, you may wish to try tackling them head on. If they are large, you would be well advised to adopt the creativity techniques outlined here.

Unlike the first step, where a number of techniques fit together in progression, all but one of these problem-solving techniques are pure alternatives. We will first look at the techniques themselves – eight in all – then consider how to select one.

Challenging assumptions

At first sight this is the most ridiculous creativity technique you are likely to come across, and for that reason could be one of the most effective. The technique is to deny a basic assumption you could make about the problem you face. Imagine a restaurant that cannot serve food, or an airline that cannot fly planes, or a tool shop with no tools.

To demonstrate this technique let us look at a long-range bus company who want to know how to expand their business. Imagine how you would cope if you were no longer able to use buses for the purpose they were built for – not an impossible scenario as transport legislation tightens. What would you do? Could you find other ways of transporting people? Could you find other uses for the buses? Could you find other uses for the garages?

Alternative methods of transport

_____

_____

_____

_____

_____

_____

Alternative uses for the equipment

_____

_____

_____

_____

_____

_____

Other ideas

_____

_____

_____

_____

_____

Scribble down as many ideas as you can; don't worry about making them sensible. When you have exhausted the various possibilities, look back at the problem statement, 'How to expand the bus company's business.' We are now replacing the challenged assumption, but keeping the ideas we developed. Which of these new ideas could you combine?

You might, for instance, have a horse and cart as an alternative method of transport. Could you combine this with bus tours to give old-time tours, offering a period feel with all the comforts of a modern bus? You might have suggested using your buses as caravans under alternative uses. What about combining this with the bus company in some way? Perhaps offer beds or sleeper seats on long journeys. Now use your ideas to make some combinations of your own.

Combinations of ideas with the bus company

_____

_____

_____

_____

_____

_____

_____

As you can see, what we are doing by denying assumptions is to force ourselves to move away the obstacle. Some of the directions we head off in will lead nowhere, but some of them will allow us to reach our goal.

Distortion

Distortion is a related technique to challenging assumptions. In this case we make a lesser change to a basic fact. This could be done by making the problem much bigger than it actually is, making it much smaller than it actually is, or by altering a fundamental characteristic of the problem area.

If we had a difficulty with communication within a small company, we could distort it by imagining that we have only one person to communicate with. What would we do to make this as effective as possible? We could equally imagine that we wished to communicate with the whole country, or even the whole world. Many of the ideas which we generate during this distortion could be altered to make them applicable to our company.

Using the distortion technique helps to come up with ideas which will support a supermarket manager who is having problems with queues at her checkout desks. Her problem statement: 'How to reduce checkout queuing time.' Imagine you can have only one checkout. How would you cope with this limitation? Next, imagine that you have a thousand checkouts. What problems does this solve? What problems does it cause?

One checkout

_____

_____

_____

_____

_____

_____

One thousand checkouts

_____

_____

_____

_____

_____

_____

Next, think through how you can combine the ideas you have generated with your original problem. Is there any way you can move towards improving the checkout queues?

Now imagine ways that you can use this technique on problems of your own. How does this technique help you to get around your obstacles?

Reversal

The final technique working on our assumptions takes the approach to the extreme. Using our earlier example of a communication problem within a company, instead of merely denying an assumption we could totally reverse it.

If we were challenging assumptions, we would say, 'What if you could not communicate?' With reversal that becomes, 'What would you do to actively ensure that there was no communication?' How would you make sure that nobody knows anything of your plans, the customers, the future of the company, the past results, or even their role in the organisation? As you can imagine this technique can be quite fun. It can also be very unsettling when you realise that the undesirable actions you list are the very things you are doing at the moment!

Try the reversal technique on something really big. Try to generate ideas which will help you to achieve a life goal. If you are overweight and want to become slimmer, imagine what you would do if you wanted to make sure that you became fatter and fatter. If you smoke and wish that you didn't, plan ways to increase, rather than reduce, your consumption of cigarettes. Or perhaps try something more positive, like learning the foreign language you have always wanted to be able to speak. In doing this, don't expect to come up with an immediate solution, but do expect to shed some light on the obstacles you are currently placing in your own path.

Life goal: _____

_____

Reversal: _____

_____

Ideas: _____

_____

_____

_____

_____

Having generated the ideas, the obvious final step is to see which of them can be reversed to help with the achievement of the life goal.

Fantasy

There cannot be many business books which recommend daydreaming. The message is often to focus, stick to the knitting, keep your nose to the grindstone, and lead a worthy, if dull, life. The messages associated with creativity are quite different. You will focus, but only after you have strayed completely from the subject. You do work hard, but only if it's fun. Fantasy is the archetypal technique in this respect. This is your opportunity to remove all real world barriers and obstacles and to day-dream. If anything could happen, how would you solve your problem?

Let's set a problem. The common household iron is inherently unsafe, particularly in a house with children where it presents all sorts of dangers. Your task is to develop ideas for a safer iron. Use fantasy to describe how you would protect children, adults, pets and your house from the dangers of the iron. Don't stick to the real world: you can use science fiction, magic or just plain silliness. The wackier the ideas the better.

How to build a safer iron: _____

_____

_____

_____

_____

_____

_____

Scribble as many ideas as you can and do not be inhibited by any sense of realism.

The next stage is to take your fantasies and move them

towards reality. For the purposes of this exercise you do not
need a solution that can be implemented, you merely need to
be able to see it heading in the right direction. Take three of
the silly ideas you wrote above and think of ways that you
could move them towards reality. You might redefine the
words you have used (a force field might become a guard or
surround); you might describe practical solutions (an iron that
disappears when danger looms might become one with a built-
in thermostat which immediately cools its outer surface if too
hot); or you might broaden the solution (an iron which works
when cold may need the development of new fabrics). Try it
now with three of your ideas.

How to   : _____

_____

_____

_____

How to   : _____

_____

_____

_____

How to   : _____

_____

_____

_____

Someone else's view

The next technique is to take someone else's view. You have seen this in action already with the historical television salesperson in the introductory section of the book (pages 21–22). In this technique you adopt the persona of another human being (or animal) whose knowledge, worries, concerns, joys and everyday experiences of life are fundamentally different from your own. You then describe your problem and solutions to your problem in terms that they would understand.

In choosing your character, make sure that there are a range of differences between you. You may choose an historical character, such as Queen Elizabeth the First; you may choose a fictional character, such as Captain Jean-Luc Picard; or you may choose someone who is merely different, such as a Turkish taxi driver. This technique is particularly good for gaining insight into your problem, as well as providing solutions which come from an unexpected angle.

In order to try out this technique we'll set a problem for you to think about: how to improve informal communication within your company. First, choose your character – remember, he or she can be historical, fictional or just plain different.

Character: _____

Now write some notes on how this character might view the problem as stated.

_____

_____

_____

_____

_____

_____

Finally, take these notes and try to relate them to the realities of the obstacles which you face. Do not make the mistake of being too down to earth at this stage. You can allow some flights of fancy.

_____

_____

_____

_____

_____

Metaphor

A powerful technique is the use of metaphor and simile (lively images and comparisons). We use metaphors and similes in our language all the time, for example when we describe an answer as being 'in the ballpark'. In framing problems, a very effective approach is to build a metaphor into the problem statement. If we can translate our problem into a metaphorical view, it can generate a whole new range of possibilities.

In the previous chapter, we described the problem of getting a boss to move from monitoring inputs to outputs. Stating this as a metaphor, we might say the problem was 'how to get my boss to weigh my output'. There's no suggestion that the boss will actually put what you produce on to a set of scales, but if we can hold that image in mind, it could generate a range of solutions which weren't apparent from the original problem statement.

Selecting the right metaphor can be tricky because some are undoubtedly more effective than others. Some are effective because they share similarities with the problem statement and so lead to immediate associations from a different field. Others are effective because they are fundamentally different and so lead to associations which are totally off the wall. For instance: my company is like an ice cream. Now think of reasons why this might be the case and list them below.

_____

_____

_____

_____

Bearing your ideas in mind, think of the ice cream (your company) melting. What might this mean? How could you stop it? What could you do if it had already melted? You can see the effect this approach has. You are thinking about your company in ways that you have not done before. If you were to spend time linking a problem to a metaphor, and then using the associations generated as a source of ideas, you would come at the problem from a very different angle to the normal, logical approach.

Random word

This technique is one of the easiest creativity techniques to apply and for this reason you may find yourself falling back on it as a mainstay. This need not be a problem, but remember that there is a larger box of tools available. Don't make the mistake of reaching for the same tool – it is easy to get stale.

In this technique you pick a word at random and then use that word to generate a plethora of associations which have nothing to do with your problem. You then relate the associations back to the problem in hand. Very often links appear as you are developing the associations. This is all to the good.

The first problem is choosing a random word. Use nouns. Ideally, use nouns which are rich in imagery. Below is a list of 60 words. You can choose one at random by looking at the second hand on your watch and picking the word in the list that corresponds to the seconds, ie if the second hand is pointing at 42 then take the forty-second word.

Sixty-second random word list

1. Fox	21. House	41. Hat
2. Car	22. Computer	42. Witch
3. Glove	23. Acrobat	43. Shovel
4. Fire engine	24. Calendar	44. Chalk board
5. Church	25. Knife	45. Door
6. Waste bin	26. Cat	46. Keyboard
7. Garage	27. Rose	47. Nuclear bomb
8. Briefcase	28. Underwear	48. Tidal wave
9. Spectacles	29. Binoculars	49. Whisky
10. Doctor	30. Sailing ship	50. Magic wand
11. Boa constrictor	31. Sculpture	51. Slot machine
12. Skateboard	32. Dolphin	52. Factory whistle
13. Running shoes	33. Book	53. Snail
14. Compact disc	34. Crayon	54. Mask
15. Glue	35. Castle	55. Flag
16. Jet plane	36. Birthday party	56. Prison
17. Postman	37. Baby	57. Television
18. Concrete	38. Magnet	58. Freezer
19. Light	39. Penguin	59. Wedding ring
20. Swing	40. Drain	60. Apple

Feel free to make up your own lists of random words if this is a technique you find useful. As long as the word conjures up an image of some sort, it is effective. At the end of a session using the random word technique, participants will often say, 'We were lucky we chose that word; it worked well for our particular problem.' This is because such words work well for any problem.

Now try the technique. Using the problem statement below, write a random word from the list (select it using your watch) and note down as many associations with that word as you can.

How to apply creativity in my everyday life.

Random word:_____

Associations:_____

_____

_____

_____

_____

Take those associations with the word and relate them back to the problem statement.

_____

_____

_____

_____

_____

Random picture

The random picture technique is exactly the same as random word, but uses a picture to stimulate the random associations. For some people it is more effective, producing a better range of ideas. Before you can use this technique you must select a random image. To get started quickly, take a well-illustrated, general interest magazine such as a Sunday colour supplement and use page numbers against seconds as we did earlier with words. Ideally, we would suggest building a collection of images. If you can collect 60, selection is easier.

Get hold of a few old magazines and catalogues and go through looking for images which evoke an emotion. In many ways, the more enigmatic the image the better. If you are able to weave a dozen different stories around the picture, it is ideal. Cut out and collect any suitable images. Number them to help with random selection.

Now choose a picture at random and look for associations. You will then apply the associations to the problem in exactly the same way as you did with the random word. Try this as your problem statement:

How to get more satisfaction out of my job.

Random picture:_____

Associations: _____

_____

_____

_____

_____

Take those associations with the picture and relate them back to the problem statement.

_____

_____

_____

_____

_____

If this technique works well for you, do consider building a small library of pictures.

A different solution

This is not really an idea-generating technique in its own right, but rather one that should be considered whichever other technique is in use. Sometimes the obstacles which stand in the way of an otherwise perfect solution are too great. In such circumstances it is quite easy to look for an alternative. But this technique can also be applied when we have an acceptable solution.

The difficulty with implementing this approach is that when most people find an initial answer to their problem, they convince themselves that it is the only possible one. Looking for a second-best solution is not regarded as a viable alternative, yet there are few problems which have only one solution. We convince ourselves that there is only a single option as a convenience. It simplifies our view of the world. Now, a bold assertion – whatever your problem, whatever the solution you intend to follow, there is another one which is almost as good and quite possibly better.

Get into the habit of writing down second- and third-best solutions and approaches to a problem.

Solution building in action

This chapter is the largest in the book and you have been asked to consider a great deal. When faced with a problem the choice of techniques is largely arbitrary. Any and all of the idea-generating techniques listed will work on large or small problems and with individuals or groups. Most creativity techniques transfer well to group settings because they allow people to let their hair down. It is important, however, that you ring the changes and use different techniques. If not, your idea generation may follow well-trodden paths and become as stale as if you had not used a creativity technique.

Whichever technique you choose, you are liable to generate a number of ideas. Try not to go for a single one immediately; remember to look for different solutions.

If you have difficulty deciding on a technique, or find yourself using the same one all the time, choose one at random. Use the second hand of your watch again, selecting one of the eight techniques by allocating the first eight blocks of seven seconds to a technique – the remaining four seconds can act as a 'throw again' section.

0–6 seconds   – Challenging assumptions
7–13 seconds   – Distortion
14–20 seconds – Reversal

21–27 seconds   —   Fantasy
28–34 seconds   —   Someone else's view
35–41 seconds   —   Metaphor
42–48 seconds   —   Random word
49–55 seconds   —   Random picture
56–59 seconds   —   Undertake a short task, then try again.

Finally, remember that procrastination is the biggest enemy of creative thought. Don't just sit there, do something! Having said that, do not be in too much of a rush. There is often benefit in allowing time for incubation of the problem. Use the techniques early by all means, but do not force yourself to close down on a solution sooner than you need. Don't just do something, sit there! The very best creative technique is to start thinking. The second best is to stop for a while.

The ideas you have generated in this step are not yet ready to see the light of day. There is work to be done to make them more robust and practical. In the next chapter we will perform a reality check on them.

CHAPTER 6
Step 3: Reality Check

By its very nature, the creative process can throw up excellent ideas which are incomplete or limited. Before implementing a solution, it is good practice to carry out a reality check to make sure the solution is viable and to refine it to a workable state. This can be a private exercise, but is even better if it can be done with a group, gathering a range of opinions.

The reality check is particularly valuable if you have taken our advice from the previous chapter and brought forward a number of possible solutions. Out of this step you will gather enough information to choose the way forward.

Gut feel

An excellent starting point is the gut feel. What do you feel about the proposed solution? It's easy to dismiss feelings as subjective and thus irrelevant, but they are very important to the way things happen in reality. No one is totally objective and we need to recognise this in the process.

The first stage of the reality check is to take a step back from the mechanics and processes of problem solving. Simply say to yourself, 'How do I feel about the idea?' What is your personal judgement, your gut feel? Let's go back to an example we generated in Chapter 2. We used the level chain to come up with the idea of selling paint in ring-pull cans (see pages

19–20). On a few lines, jot down your gut reaction to the idea. Not technical pros and cons: what do you *feel* about it?

_____

_____

_____

_____

_____

Now make use of your feelings. Do you strongly dislike the idea? If so, make sure you know why; if you dislike it, perhaps you should abandon this approach and go back to develop another one – remember, there is never a single solution. Does the idea give you a warm glow? Why? How can you make sure that these positive aspects of the solution, which you like so much, are sold to other people? Would some small change make things even better?

Stakeholders

Having established the gut feel of the most important person involved – you – it is necessary to take into account the views of the other stakeholders – the people and groups who will be influenced by your solution.

Dealing with this technique is a two-stage process. First, we have to identify the stakeholders. Review the aerial survey produced in step 1 (page 36) and distil from it any individuals, groups and companies who are going to be affected by your solution.

Try it now. Consider whatever you will be working on next. List the stakeholders on the lines below. Who will benefit? Will anyone be adversely affected? Who has to do something? Who is in charge? Who will be signing the cheque?

Stakeholders: _____

_____

_____

_____

_____

_____

_____

Once you have identified your stakeholders, the other part of the technique is to decide how they will react to your idea – what they will think of the route you have produced in the building stage. This needn't be a long process. For each principal stakeholder, write a short sentence describing their expected reactions. Put yourself in their position – try to think how they will think.

When you have your list of stakeholder views, treat them much as you have your own gut feelings, and keep the output in front of you as you work through the rest of the process.

For a large problem, you might consider taking this technique one stage further and involve your stakeholders directly by using questionnaires or interviews to gather their reaction to your idea. You will often be surprised by the outcome.

Plus points

Once we have established the feelings of those involved, we need to clarify just what is good about the proposed solution. This process is particularly useful if you are still working with a number of possibilities, but will also feed into business cases and will help to ensure that we have chosen a suitable action.

Let's carry on with the idea of paint in ring-pull cans. What's good about the idea? How do we (and the stakeholders – you'd better do a quick stakeholder exercise first) benefit? It is very important at this stage that you concentrate on the positive. There will be an opportunity to look at the bad points in a moment.

So, for paint in ring-pull cans, what are the plus points?

_____

_____

_____

_____

_____

_____

Having generated these positive aspects, make sure that they haven't indicated something not quite right about the solution, or an opportunity to develop an even better approach.

Now, forget the plus points for a moment as we move on to the dark side.

Minus points

There is no such thing as a perfect idea. To maximise the chance of a successful implementation it is important that we identify any potential snags and hazards created by our idea.

Just as we went through and looked for positive aspects, we now go through and look for what's wrong. Let's do the exercise again, using our hypothetical ring-pull paint product. What could go wrong with it? How can it cause trouble for us or our stakeholders? An ideal minus point not only says what's wrong, but how to fix it. As you come up with each point, jot down a couple of ways that the original idea could be changed to fix the problem.

So, for paint in ring-pull cans, what are the minus points?

_____

_____

_____

_____

_____

_____

_____

As a result of establishing these minus points, your original idea may now have been changed to be more practical. If you couldn't think of an appropriate remedy for the minus point, try treating it as an obstacle in its own right and applying one of the techniques from step 2 (page 39). Even if you haven't come up with an immediate solution, at least it's flagged up for when you implement the idea.

Reality check in action

This is the easiest part of the process to skip over because it is about fine tuning, but to omit the reality check is to put your idea at risk. The reality check need not take long, and it is nearly always worth using all four items in the toolkit.

What you will come out with is a modified view of your idea. You will have put on the table your own feelings and those of your stakeholders – no hidden agendas. You may have already made direct changes to the solution. You may even decide as a result of this step that you need to go back to the solution-building stage to circumvent an obstacle that you were not aware of before. If, however, you go forward positively, the reality check will have paved the way for the final step of the business creativity process: implementation.

CHAPTER 7
Step 4: Implementation

No application, no creativity

Imagine a museum dedicated to tools and machinery. It might be fascinating. It might give an insight into the way things have changed over time. But the machines and tools would not be fulfilling the functions for which they were designed. They are serving a purpose, but not as tools; they have become curios or a source of inspiration.

Creativity is a little like this. A creative idea which is not applied may be of interest, but it is not fulfilling the function for which it was designed. This is true even of an artistic concept. An idea for a beautiful sculpture which is never realised may be exciting, but it is not yet doing what the artist intended. Implementation is about turning creative ideas and problem solutions into reality.

Have you ever had an idea that you didn't follow through? If you are anything like the rest of the population you will have had hundreds, even thousands, of unfulfilled ideas. Try to think of a few of them now and list them overleaf. If you cannot think of any you have had in the past, come up with some new ideas now. It doesn't matter how off the wall they may be, just list them.

_____

_____

_____

_____

_____

_____

_____

_____

Some of your ideas (not necessarily the ones above) could have made a significant difference to your life if only you had done something with them. This chapter should help to make that happen in the future.

Implementation style

We will look at the implementation toolkit in a moment, but first we need to establish the different possible approaches. As we remarked earlier, there is a distinct danger in trying to take the same approach for all types of problem. Are you in control or is someone else? Do you see an obvious way forward? Is this exercise the most important thing you are doing or merely a part of a whole set of other objectives? We have classified problems into four types: the clear problem, the diffuse problem, the managed problem and the background problem. Each has its own characteristics and will need a different mix of the toolkit to implement a solution for it.

The clear problem
This is a problem where the actions you need to take are obvious. It may still be a big problem, but it is amenable to rigorous analysis and a structured implementation. You need only be aware of the milestones you pass in order to track the progress of your solution. You are very much in control of actions. Here implementation is primarily about monitoring the progress of a project where there is no doubt about the path to be followed.

The diffuse problem
With a problem like this, your solution is much less clear cut. You know what your goals are, and your principal, intermediate milestones, but the implementation itself requires much more management concentration, focusing on the day-to-day detail of the project. The important point to remember about such an implementation is that there is nothing inherently wrong about the diffuse nature of the problem. It is, in fact, a more natural problem – almost all clear problems are to some degree artificial.

The managed problem
Here, someone else is actually undertaking the running of the project. The implementation of your idea is out of your hands, but you have a responsibility for, or an involvement in, the outcome. Examples of this type of problem would include projects where you have delegated the implementation process and want to track progress, or those where the implementation is in the hands of another agency.

The background problem
In referring to this as a background problem, we are not suggesting that it is unimportant. In fact, many of the most significant problems in your life – ones of lifestyle and career, for example – will be background problems. However, by their very nature, these are problems which are liable to take place in the background of your planning.

Here, you are in no hurry. The journey is being made for the pleasure of the trip as much as arriving at the destination. You are in control more than anyone else, but you are moved by the current of outside forces. You will still set goals and measure progress, but this implementation style is usually much longer term. Examples of this type of implementation would include learning a foreign language or starting a new business from scratch.

Having described the different types of problem, we will look at the tools at your disposal for implementation, before recommending how to use them in each case.

The implementation toolkit

The basic plan
At the end of step one we established a clear statement of the problem. In the next two steps, we built and refined a solution. Now that we are undertaking implementation we must always keep in view just what the problem is and how we are trying to solve it.

For most implementations you will need a basic plan. This comes down to asking the right questions. The questions themselves are simple: What, Why, Where, When, Who, and How?

What: do I want to achieve?
resources do I need?
Why: do I want to do it?
Where: do I want to do it?
When: do I need to start?
do I need to finish?
Who: can I use to do the work?
will be responsible for different aspects?
can I call on for help?
How: do I go about doing it?

Some of the techniques below help to provide answers to these questions for larger, more complex projects. It is also worth highlighting what resources are at your disposal, both for regular use and when implementation hits a snag.

Equipment and contingencies

Whether we are talking about actual physical equipment needed to implement your solution – a PC or a bulldozer – or metaphorical equipment – the capabilities and experience of your people – the time to discover that you don't have the right equipment is before you start the implementation, not when you are half way to failure.

Before you do anything else, list the resources, the talents, the capabilities you will need. One essential point is to be aware of what you have available in the event of contingencies. You may need a way to call in help – how would you go about it? When considering 'Who?' resources, think about who might be able to pull you out of the mire if everything goes wrong. How do you involve them?

A significant part of thinking through the plan is being aware of the equipment and resources which you will need, and the stages of the project at which you will need them. Start this planning early.

Planning techniques

Developing a project plan is vital to the success of any implementation. Whether you are spending a few minutes of your spare time and the plan has just an arbitrary time limit, or whether the implementation takes over your life and your office is filled with Gantt charts (see page 70). The plan is best represented as a pictorial overview of the implementation.

For long projects you will need plans working to different timescales, beginning with the overview planner and zooming in to progressively more detailed plans as you near completion. You might also need to detail points along the way which can act as intermediate deliveries when the overall implementation is too large to cope with in its entirety.

Planning is the most critical implementation tool available to you. This book is not the place to give you details of all of the project planning techniques which you might want to learn about. Below there is a brief list which is intended merely to give an overview. If you are responsible for managing a large implementation project, you will need to do further work to learn about and be able to use these techniques. For most implementation exercises many of them will be overkill and the brief introduction given here will suffice.

Task list or schedule

By far the simplest planning technique is to list the activities required and the time and resources which the activities will consume. It takes a few minutes to complete such a list and for any implementation which takes more than an hour or two itself it would be a foolish step to miss.

Mind map

For implementations which are unclear you will probably find mind mapping useful. (Mind mapping was covered in the aerial survey section of Chapter 4.) Make a mind map of your goal, bringing into it the stakeholders, resources, obstacles to overcome, and timings both desired and imposed.

Gantt chart

A Gantt chart is a bar chart which lays out the critical steps in the project against timescales. The time is usually the horizontal axis, the tasks are listed on the vertical axis and a bar is drawn in the chart to represent the work undertaken. Figure 7.1 is an example of a Gantt chart for a project to sew a patchwork quilt. In this example the activities follow on from one another, but there is no reason that some could not happen simultaneously.

The Gantt chart is particularly useful for working out how resources are to be deployed, and what the requirements of a particular project are.

Arrow or network chart

This is a chart where the activities are represented as arrows which link the major events. Such charts form the basis of critical path analysis and Figure 7.2 provides an example.

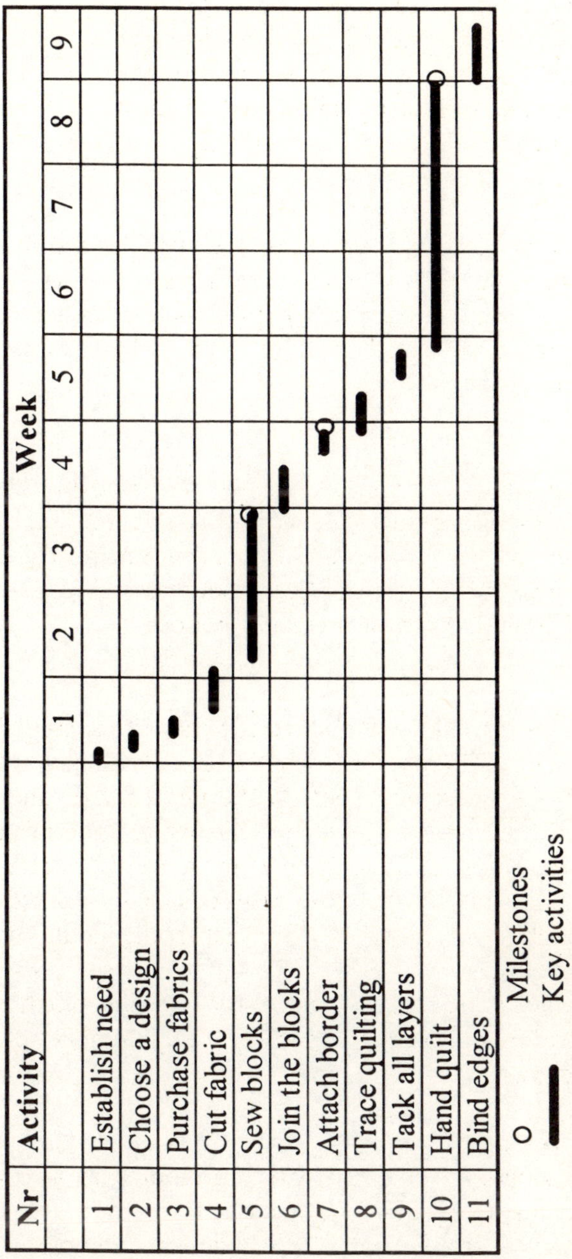

Nr	Activity	Week								
		1	2	3	4	5	6	7	8	9
1	Establish need									
2	Choose a design									
3	Purchase fabrics									
4	Cut fabric									
5	Sew blocks									
6	Join the blocks									
7	Attach border									
8	Trace quilting									
9	Tack all layers									
10	Hand quilt									
11	Bind edges									

O   Milestones

━━   Key activities

Figure 7.1 *A Gantt chart*

71

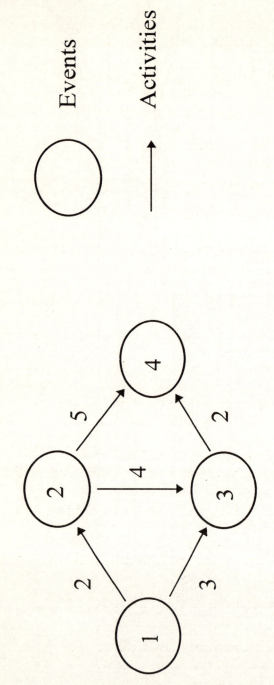

Figure 7.2 *An arrow or network chart*

The numbers in the circles represent the sequence number of the event. The numbers beside the arrows represent the length of time taken for the activities. Each event should have a higher number than any event which precedes it.

Once you have drawn an arrow chart, you can look for the path which determines the earliest completion time of the highest numbered event. In Figure 7.2 it is clear that this path is determined by the event sequence 1, 2, 3, 4. The time to complete this path will be $2 + 4 + 2$ units. This means that the earliest we can complete event 4 is 8 units of time from the start.

The calculation of critical paths, slack and event times in more complex charts is worthy of further research. As charts become more complex it is worth considering one of the many project planning software packages now available to simplify this process.

This is a technique which becomes much easier and clearer with practice. Take a project or hobby with which you are very familiar and draw an arrow chart like the one in Figure 7.2. Having assigned times to the activities, calculate the critical path from the start event to the finish event.

The arrow chart is particularly useful to get a feel for time constraints and where milestones should be placed.

How?

This is really a variation on the 'Why?' approach used in step one (see page 30). Now that we are implementing an idea, it is useful to repetitively ask 'How?'.

As an example of this, take one of the ideas you listed at the start of this chapter and just keep asking and re-asking 'How?'.

Idea: _____

_____

How?_____

_____

How? _____

_____

How? _____

_____

How? _____

_____

The 'How?' technique is one to pull out of the toolbox when you are not sure where to start with a plan. By refining your requirement, you should get a clearer picture of the way forward.

Milestones

The tracking of progress during implementation is vital. Whichever style of problem you are handling, measuring progress is one of the most important features of your ability to control the implementation.

When you have decided which implementation techniques you are going to use and have drawn an initial plan, allow yourself some time to add milestones to it. If someone else is running the project, they may decide on the milestones and your role is then to monitor them as they occur. If you are in charge, you must decide which events are critical and when they need to be monitored. Do not stack all of your milestones at the end of an implementation: space them evenly throughout. Don't allow slippage on the early milestones in the belief that you will catch up later − you will not catch up without significant additional effort.

Intermediate goals

If your implementation is over a long period, you will need intermediate goals. These are very similar to milestones but they are larger and represent a significant deliverable in themselves. You can pass by a milestone, but for an intermediate goal you will want to pat yourself on the back, take stock and spend some time detailing the next section of the implementation.

You will plan where you want to be at each intermediate goal. Having set out the plan, decide which events are key, in particular those with concrete deliverables, and set the completion of a few of these as intermediate goals. Make sure that they are spaced evenly throughout the journey.

At each goal take stock of your progress. How well are you progressing against plan, against budget, and against best and worst that could happen? What slack do you have ahead of you in the process? Are the critical path items being completed on schedule? Have any unforeseen bottlenecks occurred? If you are using a technique to represent your plan graphically, you may want to expand the detail around the intermediate goal, as well as producing a detailed plan for the next section of your implementation.

Implementation in action

Putting implementation into action first involves deciding on the sort of problem you are dealing with. Categorise it as clear, diffuse, managed or background. Make sure that you have your problem statement clearly in mind. Below are suggestions for the techniques which would be most appropriate for each of these problem types. Remember that there are no hard-and-fast rules. What you do and how you do it depends upon the size of your project, the timescales, the degree of control you have and, above all, what you want.

Clear

Basic plan: Write this for every implementation.

Equipment and contingency:	Since you are in control, you must think this through. If your implementation is significant, you would benefit from writing down detail of equipment and contingencies.
Planning techniques:	The degree to which you plan out a clear problem depends upon the time that the project will take and its level of complexity. Any of the planning techniques could be useful. Don't forget that you can plan your intermediate goals in detail.
Milestones:	For any type of implementation, think through the milestones.
Intermediate goals:	Plan intermediate goals carefully. You may want to celebrate them. Take stock of progress at each completion.

Diffuse

Basic plan:	Write this for every implementation.
Equipment and contingency:	You must think this through even more than with a clear problem. If your implementation is significant, you would benefit from writing down details. You will definitely want to think about who you would call for help and how you would get it if your project is of any size. Remember, when the problem is diffuse you are more likely to stray from plan and need help.
Planning techniques:	As with a clear problem, the degree of planning will depend upon the length of the project and its complexity. The more complex, the more plans you should draw. Don't forget to plan intermediate goals in detail.
Milestones:	For any type of implementation, think through the milestones.
Intermediate goals:	Plan intermediate goals carefully. You may want to celebrate them. Take stock of progress at each completion.

Managed

Basic plan:	Write this for every implementation.
Equipment and contingency:	These should be provided for you; your involvement in planning is minimal.
Planning techniques:	You will probably not need to develop your own plans but be aware of those drawn up by the project leader.
Milestones:	For any type of implementation, think through the milestones.
Intermediate goals:	If the implementation is long, plan where you intend to stop and take stock. Find out from the person managing the project what intermediate goals they have planned: you should have an input.

Background

Basic plan:	Write this for every implementation.
Equipment and contingency:	Think about what you will need as you progress through your implementation, but don't be afraid to amend the resources you require (or other aspects of your plan) as you progress. You will want to think about who you can call on for help, but you will not often need it in a hurry.
Planning techniques:	For a background problem of any length, you must produce plans. These may be simple mind maps, but some form of written or pictorial representation of your implementation will increase the chances of success.
Milestones:	For any type of implementation, think through the milestones.
Intermediate goals:	Solutions to background problems tend to have long implementations. Plan plenty of intermediate goals, to take stock and keep up morale.

The whole implementation

To practise the application of these techniques there are four examples below, one for each problem style, which will allow you to apply them with no risk.

Clear
You have the job of designing a training course for a computer software package or trainable skill which you know well. Write out the plan and a list of possible milestones and intermediate goals.

Diffuse
Ann and Jane are friends who want to set up a small mail order business together. They can only work on it in the evenings at the moment, but would like to move to full-time employment and eventually even to hiring staff. Draw a mind map to shown an overview of their implementation. What contingency support do they have at their disposal and how would they get it?

Managed
You have hired a consultant to install a computer system and to train your staff. Draw a plan of the process showing the milestones and intermediate goals.

Background
Mary Jones, 45, has bought a small cottage in the country as a future retirement home. She is spending weekends decorating and gardening but it is still a long way from being a home. Either plan her implementation or describe and plan one of your own – perhaps the one you generated in the reversal exercise in Chapter 2 (pages 45–46).

CHAPTER 8
Regular Creativity

Creativity-driven exercise

As we saw in the previous chapter, creativity is not an end in itself. Equally, learning creativity techniques has little value unless you put them into practice. The key to getting real benefit from creativity is to use it regularly and frequently.

This can be approached from two directions, and ideally you should attempt both at once (a concept which is quite creative in itself, as most people find it difficult to approach anything from two directions at once). The first line of attack is to undertake a mechanical, diary-driven procedure, independent of the particular problems you have at the moment. Set aside a short time on a regular basis for creative thinking.

The difficulty here is not the actual creativity, but ever getting started. This will not work unless you sit down now with your diary and block off personal creativity sessions. It need not be a huge commitment. Try booking a 15-minute session, once a week. Pick a part of the day and the week when you are on your best form and unlikely to be disturbed: for one of us it happens to be first thing in the morning; for the other lunchtime is best. Bearing in mind your regular commitments, when would be a good time?

Write it on the line below (eg 8.30 am, each Wednesday morning).

_____

While the commitment is still fresh in your mind, put it in your diary for the next month – and with the last entry, remind yourself to extend it another month.

When your personal creativity session comes around, let any problem or decision or idea generation you are involved with pop into your mind. Don't worry whether it is a work or home activity. In your 15 minutes, work quickly through the four steps. Don't try to do anything in detail. Spend three or four minutes on each stage. You will be surprised how much progress you can often make.

We often stress; sometimes you won't get anywhere, but those wasted 15 minutes will be far outweighed by the benefits of the other sessions. You can also look on them as creative workouts; as long as you've built up a mental sweat, you've done some good.

Make sure you choose a different subject each week. If that sounds like a lot of problems, don't worry. You've got plenty – we all have. Before proceeding further with this chapter, have a practice session. If now isn't an appropriate time, at least make sure you've scheduled one.

Problem-driven exercise

The regular creativity session will help keep your creative muscles in trim, but the other way you need to sustain your use of creativity is in the everyday work you undertake. When you are setting out to start something new, when you are looking to solve a problem, when something unexpected pops up, don't plunge in and try to fight your way to an instant solution. Step back for a second. Decide how much of the four-step process you would like to apply, and begin to use it. As soon as you have plunged into a task thinking, 'This is too important/too rushed/too insignificant to worry about using creativity', you have taken a step towards losing the battle. When you are taking on a new challenge get in the habit of seeing how creativity fits in – it will almost always improve the outcome.

A checklist

We have emphasised all along that we are not providing a rigid structure, but rather a memory-jogging framework to help you apply creativity. This checklist should help you pull in the right elements when faced with a new problem or task.

Information surveying
- [ ] Problem statement – 'How to ...' statement
- [ ] Why – refined the problem: asked 'Why?' several times
  Choose a problem-identifying technique
  - [ ] Obstacle map – Where are you, where do you want to get to – for problems?
  - [ ] Level chain – moved up and down levels – for new ideas
- [ ] Aerial survey – collected information, mind map drawn.

Building a solution
- [ ] Select a technique
  - [ ] challenging assumptions
  - [ ] distortion
  - [ ] reversal
  - [ ] fantasy
  - [ ] another person
  - [ ] metaphor
  - [ ] random word
  - [ ] random picture
- [ ] Consider alternative solution(s)
- [ ] For a significant problem, go back and try another technique to widen solution options.

Reality check
- [ ] What's your gut feeling?

☐ Identified stakeholders, and their probable views
☐ What are the good points of the idea?
☐ What are the bad points of the idea? How to fix them.

Implementation
☐ Type of problem identified
    ☐ clear
    ☐ diffuse
    ☐ managed
    ☐ background
☐ Plan written
☐ Equipment and contingencies
    If this is a large project:
    ☐ Planning techniques used
        ☐ Task list
        ☐ Mind map
        ☐ Gantt chart
        ☐ Arrow chart
        ☐ How?
☐ Milestones positioned
    If this is a large project:
    ☐ Intermediate goals positioned
☐ Understand the whole implementation?
☐ Make it happen.

And finally ...

This has been a brief summary of creativity. There are many more techniques available which fit comfortably within the framework. We selected those which we use most frequently and most effectively. You might well have read this book without attempting any of the exercises in the belief that you will learn about creativity just as effectively. If this is the case, you will have missed out. Do go back and run through the exercises. It will not take much time. Not doing the exercises will save you a few minutes; doing them will pay handsome dividends which will make those few minutes seem insignificant by comparison.

The final section of the book contains references which you may wish to follow up to learn more about creativity and creativity techniques. We hope that you have enjoyed the book, and we hope even more that you get as much pleasure from using these ideas as we do.

References

Alan Baddeley, *Your Memory: A User's Guide*, Penguin Books, London, 1994

Edward de Bono, *Lateral Thinking*, Pelican Books, Harmondsworth, 1977

Edward de Bono, *Serious Creativity*, HarperCollins, London, 1993

Tony Buzan, *Use Your Head*, BBC Books, London, 1982

Tony and Barry Buzan, *The Mind Map Book*, BBC Books, London, 1993

Carol Kinsey Goman, *Creative Thinking in Business*, Kogan Page, London, 1989

Jane Henry, *Creative Management*, Sage Publications Ltd, London, 1993

James M Higgins, *101 Creative Problem Solving Techniques*, New Management Publishing Co Inc, New York, 1994

Arthur Koestler, *The Act of Creation*, Pan Books, London, 1966

Philip Kotler, *Marketing Management*, Prentice Hall, New Jersey, 1984

Michael Michalko, *Thinkertoys*, Ten Speed Press, Berkeley, CA, 1991

Roger von Oech, *A Whack on the Side of the Head*, Warner Books, New York, 1983

Roger von Oech, *A Kick in the Seat of the Pants*, Harper & Row, New York, 1986

Alex F Osborn, *Applied Imagination*, Charles Scribner's Sons, New York, 1963

Tom Peters, *The Tom Peters Seminar*, Macmillan, London, 1994

Peter Russell, *The Brain Book*, Routledge & Kegan Paul, London, 1985

Roger G Schroeder, *Operations Management*, McGraw-Hill, Maidenhead, 1981

Trevor L Young, *Implementing Projects*, The Industrial Society, London, 1993